Simple Solutions™

Aggression

By
Kim Campbell Thornton
Illustrations by Buck Jones

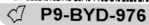

Plus Training Tips

BOWTIE PRESS®

IRVINE, CALIFORNIA

Nick Clemente, Special Consultant
Karla Austin, Business Operations Manager
Ruth Strother, Editor-at-Large
Michelle Martinez, Editor
Michael Vincent Capozzi, Designer

The dogs in this book are referred to as *he* and *she* in alternating chapters.

Library of Congress Cataloging-in-Publication Data

Thornton, Kim Campbell.
  Simple solutions : aggression / by Kim Campbell Thornton ;
illustrations by Buck Jones.
     p. cm.
  ISBN 1-889540-83-8 (pbk. : alk. paper)
 1. Dogs--Behavior. 2. Dogs--Training. I. Title.

  SF433.T54 2003
  636.7'0887--dc21
                                    2003004491

BowTie Press®
A Division of BowTie, Inc.
3 Burroughs
Irvine, California 92618
949-855-8822

Printed and Bound in Singapore
10 9 8 7 6 5 4 3 2

Contents

Aggression

Aggression is the most common problem canine behaviorists see. Why is it so common? The reason is simple: aggression is a normal behavior for dogs. One of the many ways dogs communicate is through actions, including threats and attacks, directed toward people or other animals. Problems with aggression occur when there's miscommunication between people and dogs—not surprising since we don't speak the same language.

Can any dog be aggressive? Yes, from toy breeds to terriers, any dog has the potential for aggression. But like it

or not, some breeds are more likely than others to have

aggressive tendencies. Terriers, for instance, have all been bred for aggression toward small, furry prey animals such as moles, badgers, and rats. When the terrier's natural prey is unavailable, this aggressive tendency can easily be turned toward cats or pocket pets such as hamsters and gerbils. Dogs who are bred to guard property or livestock have a genetic tendency toward aggression. It's a normal part of being a guard dog. Because there's genetic variability within each breed, some dogs within a breed can have a higher genetic tendency to be aggressive than others of the same breed. Because aggression is heritable, dogs who show inappropriate aggressive behavior should

be spayed or neutered so they don't pass on the tendency to their offspring.

Even though aggression is a normal behavior for dogs, it doesn't mean it should be permitted. Dogs live in a human environment and they need to learn to behave properly in that setting. It's important to understand that a dog's perceptions influence his aggressive behavior, but it's also important for dogs to be able to adjust to their living situation. In the following chapters, we'll see how to identify aggression, recognize and prevent different types of aggression, and seek solutions to aggression problems.

What Does Aggression Look Like?

Some people bring their dog to a behaviorist for being aggressive when the dog's merely jumping up on people. Jumping up is bad manners, but it's not necessarily an aggressive behavior unless the behavior is accompanied by another physical sign. An aggressive dog gives threat signals by curling her lips, baring her teeth, growling, barking threateningly, snapping, or biting. These behaviors can be directed toward people or other animals. When a dog is jumping up on someone and displaying one or more of these signals, then you have an aggressive dog.

Canine body language isn't always clear. For instance, dogs often bare their teeth in a smile or growl in play. How can you tell the difference between playing and aggressive posturing? Look at the dog's body language. If the

dog's lip retracts upward (vertically) and her body is stiff and quivering, watch out! If the lip retracts horizontally and the dog's tail is wagging, it's generally a friendly smile.

The same is true of play growls. A puppy who lifts her lip and growls while staring at you isn't showing any intent to play. On the other hand, if she's in a play bow (rear up in the air, tail wagging, head down, smiling up at you) with a happy face, you can be reasonably sure the pup is inviting you to join in on a game. Playful growls or excited barking often accompany the play bow. Once you learn how to watch dogs, you can see a clear difference between play and aggression with intent to harm. Think of it this way: if the behavior makes you want to back away from the dog—it's aggression.

Bully Boy or Fearful Fido?

Aggression can be placed in three broad categories: aggression toward owners, aggression toward strangers, and aggression toward other animals. Each has a variety of potential causes, although when you get right down to it, the main motivation for all is some form of fear.

Dogs may be aggressive toward their people because they don't understand their place in the family "pack" or they're afraid a new family member such as a baby or a new spouse threatens their place in the pack. This is often called dominance aggression, although some behaviorists are moving away from that term. Instead, they refer to it as conflict aggression because many dogs who are described as dominant also show fear. When we use the term dominant, it makes us more likely to punish a dog, which is counterproductive.

A dog with conflict aggression often hasn't learned that you and other family members are in charge and therefore tries to claim the role of leader of the pack. He might growl if asked to move off the furniture or if any attempt is made to restrain him. This dog doesn't like having his head patted because he views it as an aggressive move. You should suspect this type of aggression if your dog displays body language such as standing tall and staring at you or snarling. Other signs of conflict aggression include guarding food or favorite toys; snarling or snapping when told *no!* or when being handled for any reason; and being

overprotective of a particular family member. Conflict

aggression usually appears during adolescence and young

adulthood, which ranges from one to three years of age.

Other dogs may show aggression toward their owners because they're afraid or they associate the owner with a frightening experience—one the owner might not even be aware of. A fearful dog is often this way because he wasn't socialized properly as a puppy. It's easy to tell if a dog is fearful by reading his body language. Fearful dogs slink, crouch, shake, or cower. Don't be fooled by this behavior! If you reach for a dog and he feels cornered, he may bite. Punishment for this behavior can make a dog become even more fearful, continuing the cycle of aggression.

Dogs who are aggressive toward strangers usually behave that way because they're defending their territory, which could be the house, the yard, or the car. If your dog urine-marks—lifts his leg on trees, walls, or other objects—when you go for walks around the block, he may view the whole neighborhood as his territory. Territorial aggression is especially common when your dog is faced with unexpected or unknown people or animals.

Another type of territorial aggression is protective aggression. Protective aggression occurs when your dog is aggressive toward strangers because he thinks he needs

to protect you from an approaching stranger, especially

one on an unfamiliar vehicle such as a bicycle or a skateboard. You can put the bite on territorial aggression by taking your new puppy to puppy kindergarten classes. You can start this when your puppy is as young as 10 weeks old. When a young dog is exposed early on to lots of other people and dogs, he is less likely to become territorially aggressive.

Fear can also cause aggression toward strangers. For instance, your dog may be fearful at the veterinary clinic or grooming shop. That's why it's always a good idea for you and your dog to first visit the vet or groomer just for fun, without any painful vaccinations or scary blow dryers.

Aggression toward other animals might involve a dispute over dominance among dogs in the same household or predatory aggression toward prey animals such as cats, squirrels, or birds. Terriers love to chase cats and squirrels, and spaniels and retrievers have been known to watch pet birds for hours, waiting for a chance to pounce. Some behaviorists say this type of predatory behavior isn't really aggression at all because it's only natural for dogs—especially certain breeds—to want to catch and eat prey; you might say it's bred in the bone. Because predatory behavior is so strong in some dogs, prevention is more important than treatment. The only way to prevent preda-tory behavior is to limit the dog's opportunities to give chase. Keep your dog on a leash and under con-trol any time there's a chance he might encounter a cat or other prey animal that you don't want him to chase.

Other Types of Aggression

Some behaviorists break aggression down further, depending on how or to whom the behavior is displayed. The following are some of the many ways aggression is described. As with the types of aggression discussed earlier, they all relate back to fear in one way or another.

Possessive aggression occurs when dogs guard objects such as food, toys, or anything else they value. It's closely related to territorial and protective aggression. This is one of the easier forms of aggression to manage, which you

can do by teaching your dog that good things come when she gives up a toy or food bowl without a fight. First you combine taking an item away with giving something back. For instance, a behaviorist might recommend first adding food to your dog's dish, then taking the dish away, adding more food, and giving the dish back. The dog learns that good things happen when people touch her food dish. You can also teach your dog that if she gives up or drops a toy, another toy or a food treat appears.

Maternal aggression is the protective behavior of a mother in defense of her pups. A dog may growl or oth-

erwise act aggressively when strangers—or even favorite family members—approach her new puppies. Maternal aggression usually disappears once pups are weaned. In the meantime, though, it's important to teach Mom that it's okay for people to handle her babies, providing positive reinforcement every time she lets people approach and touch her pups. Maternal aggression is usually seen during the first three weeks after the mother dog gives birth. If she shows aggression when strangers are around, keep them away during this time. If the aggression continues after three weeks, take your dog to another room when people come to visit or take the puppies to the visitor. Puppies need socialization from people other than family members, so don't give in to maternal aggression.

Fear aggression is defensive in nature. A dog who thinks she's in danger will try to either defend herself or run—the "fight or flight" response. Dogs who haven't been well socialized might mistake innocent actions—the fast-moving hand of a toddler or an arm raised to throw a ball—as attacks and act to defend themselves by growling or biting. When they see that their behavior gets the reaction they want—a person backs off—a pattern is set. Fear aggression is often described as a kind of anxiety disorder and is treated as such. Sometimes drug therapy may help.

Pain-related aggression is exactly what it sounds like. Just as we might yell at someone who handles us roughly when we don't feel good, dogs with injuries or health problems may growl or bite when they're touched in a sore spot. Dogs who do this need to learn that touch is rewarding, not painful. Be careful any time you touch a dog in pain, and make sure your dog has plenty of handling from puppyhood on. She should be used to having you groom her, touch her feet, and look in her mouth. Teach her to let other people touch her as well. It makes it easier for veterinarians and groomers to do their jobs.

Who Ya Gonna Call?

If your dog shows signs of aggression, don't shrug it off. Aggression is a serious problem that should be dealt with immediately before the dog becomes dangerous. A single bite can scar a child for life and a more vicious attack can kill a person. In some communities, a single bite—even if it's relatively harmless—can result in the dog being euthanized. Teaching a dog to interact appropriately with people is one of a dog owner's highest responsibilities. Don't hesitate to seek professional help in countering aggressive tendencies. And until you can get help, avoid situations that seem to provoke your dog's aggressive behavior.

Begin by taking your dog to the veterinarian to rule out pain-related aggression. Your veterinarian can perform a physical exam and run lab tests to make sure your dog isn't unhealthy or in pain from an injury. If your dog is healthy, ask your veterinarian for a referral to a behaviorist. The vet may recommend a board-certified veterinary behaviorist— a vet who specializes in animal behavior—or an applied animal behaviorist certified through the Applied Animal Behavior Society. Another way to find qualified help is to

contact the American Veterinary Society of Animal Behavior at www.avma.org/avsab/ for a referral.

Even if you get a referral, look for signs that the behaviorist is up-to-date on the latest thinking in dog behavior. For instance, run from anyone who recommends alpha rolls—holding the dog on his back and staring at him—or other dominance behaviors to put the dog in his place. Alpha rolls and similar techniques are outmoded. Punishment and domination techniques almost always make aggression worse because they increase the level of fear in an already fearful dog.

Developing a treatment plan for a behavioral problem involves obtaining an accurate behavioral history to reach a precise diagnosis. At your first meeting, the behaviorist will ask you what triggers your dog's aggressive behavior. It's important that you don't leave anything out. Even minor details can help the behaviorist determine an accurate diagnosis. Depending on the diagnosis, behavior modification, environmental adjustments, or sometimes drug therapy is used to treat the aggression.

Dealing with Aggression

Behavior modification under the guidance of a qualified behaviorist is the best way to reprogram an aggressive dog. Behavior modification involves changing the dog's environment, changing the dog's behavior through training or operant conditioning (the association formed between a behavior and a consequence), or changing the dog's brain chemistry through use of drugs. Behaviorists use a variety of techniques to help dogs understand their place in the family and to learn to accept you as the leader.

These techniques include desensitizing the dog to whatever causes her fear or to the targets of the dog's aggression; withdrawing or rationing attention; teaching the dog that family members are the source of all good things; reducing the dog's sense of importance; obedience training; use of training tools such as head collars; and spaying or neutering. Be aware that there's no "one size fits all" solution. A behaviorist tailors methods to the individual dog and family situation as well as to the type of aggression. Let's take a look at one of the ways the various types of aggression might be handled.

Avoidance is the first step when treating many types of aggression. This means changing or avoiding anything that triggers the behavior. For instance, if your dog reacts aggressively when her head is patted, don't pat her head.

Why does avoidance work? It works because your dog can no longer use those situations to manipulate you and isn't being rewarded for misbehavior. And a reward is exactly what happens when you back away from your dog or stop requiring her to do something she doesn't want to do. Once your dog's ability to manipulate matters to her satisfaction is removed, behavior modification techniques can be used to change her actions and teach her to live compatibly with you and other family members.

Changing a Dog's Behavior

Behavior modification techniques can be passive or active. Passive techniques don't involve any kind of force or physical manipulation. They include ignoring the dog (no touching, or other attention); requiring the dog to work for attention or food; and not permitting the dog on any furniture or to jump up on people. All of these techniques communicate to the dog that he's no longer in charge.

How do they work? The behaviorist might start by advising you to ignore all of your dog's attempts to get your attention, such as nosing you for petting, placing a paw on your knee, or bringing a toy for play. Dogs love attention, so when it's withdrawn, they sit up and take notice.

Once you've established a pattern of withholding attention—which might take a week or two—the behaviorist might recommend that you begin to offer attention on your own terms. For instance, the behaviorist might recommend that you occasionally respond to your dog's requests for attention by first requiring him to perform a command such as *sit* or *down*. When the dog complies, give him praise, pets, and a treat. Soon your dog will learn

that rewards come with calm, attentive behavior. Even

young puppies can learn to sit still for a few seconds and

pay attention to their people when they discover that the reward is attention or food.

When you require a dog to sit or lie down before you pet him, feed him, or take him for a walk, you establish yourself as the leader. You can further establish your leadership by not letting your dog sleep on the bed, lie on furniture, or jump up on people. How can you avoid these behaviors? Take jumping up, for instance. When your dog does this, simply pivot so he misses you and then walk away. An alternative to walking away is to give the *sit* command. When the dog sits, then he gets attention.

Supervising and restricting where the dog goes are other forms of passive behavior modification. For instance, a dog who chases people or other animals in a predatory way should be confined to a yard or kept on a leash so he can't act on his instincts. Never leave this type of dog alone with babies, toddlers, or young children. In fact, no dog should ever be left unsupervised with young children.

Active behavior modification involves the use of training tools such as head collars, obedience training classes, and desensitization and counterconditioning techniques. A head collar, similar to a horse halter, allows you to control your dog's head and helps reduce pulling on walks. It's an effective, harmless way to communicate to your dog what

you want. When your dog walks nicely, then he gets praise.

Obedience training reinforces that the person is in charge. Teaching your dog to respond to commands enables you to interrupt aggressive acts and replace them with positive actions for which the dog can be rewarded. *Sit* and *down* commands are especially useful because they place the dog in a submissive position. Practice obedience work, accompanied by such positive rewards as treats, toys, or play, daily throughout your dog's life. Always end training sessions on a high note, and never ask a dog to do something he's not fully capable of achieving.

Once your dog reliably performs obedience commands—especially the *stay* command—the behaviorist may introduce desensitization and counterconditioning sessions. Desensitization and counterconditioning work by gradually exposing the dog to things that previously caused aggressive behavior and rewarding him for tolerating them. This way, the dog slowly learns to accept, strangers, cats, or whatever else he fears or dislikes. During these sessions, a muzzle may be necessary to prevent bites.

Territorial aggression is a good example of how desensitization and counterconditioning might be used. A common way of dealing with territorial aggression is to place your dog on a leash and require him to sit every time someone walks by your house. Praise him and give a treat every time he complies. Then have the dog sit, and reward him as a family member approaches the door and knocks. When this is accepted, ask a familiar neighbor to approach and knock. Repeat the sit-and-reward sequence each time he complies. Finally, work with the dog as a stranger approaches and knocks at the door. The goal is for the dog to welcome the arrival of people because he associates their approach with a treat or other reward.

Whether recommending active or passive behavior modification techniques, the behaviorist should demonstrate everything he or she asks you to do. Don't be afraid to ask questions if you don't understand something. You should also consider keeping a diary of your dog's behavior. This will help you recognize patterns and see changes. Sometimes it doesn't seem as if a dog is improving, but a look at the diary may show significant improvement so gradual that it wasn't even noticed.

Can Drugs Help?

Almost all of us would like to be able to cure problems with a pill, but medication isn't the best or most effective treatment for a complex behavior such as aggression. Drug therapy is useful for some types of aggression but not for all, and it must always be combined with behavior modification. Drugs such as Prozac and Valium have their place in dealing with behavior problems, but they're not cure-alls. There's always a risk that drugs can make aggression worse. Drugs are expensive and since the amount of the

drug given is based on a dog's size, it can cost more to treat medium-size and large dogs than small dogs. Be aware, too, that none of the drugs currently prescribed for aggression is approved for that use.

That said, drug therapy has its uses from short-term relief of anxiety during behavior modification to long-term use for hard-core cases. Several types of drugs may be prescribed for aggression. They include anxiolytics (drugs that relieve anxiety) such as buspirone or tricyclic antidepressants; specific serotonin reuptake inhibitors—SSRIs—which may reduce aggressive or impulsive behavior; or synthetic progestins, which are sometimes useful in dealing with conflict or territorial aggression but have long-term side effects.

It's important to remember that drugs aren't necessarily a quick fix. It can take six to eight weeks before any change appears in your dog's behavior. Some behaviorists recommend behavior modification before introducing drugs. That way they can see what's working and have a better idea of whether drugs can be useful.

Diet and Exercise

Diet and exercise may well be factors in dealing with aggression, and you can make some easy changes that might help reduce your dog's aggression. Since food allergies can cause behavior problems and irritability, begin by taking a look at your dog's diet. First give your dog a food with different ingredients, ideally ingredients that your dog hasn't eaten before, such as duck, turkey, or venison. Check the label on dog treats. Many are high in sugar, salt, and preservatives, which some dogs are sensitive to.

If your dog eats a diet that is high in protein—a source of energy—but leads a couch potato lifestyle, diet combined with lack of exercise may be the problem. Ask your veterinarian to recommend high-quality foods that are lower in protein. Then add some exercise to your dog's life. Putting him out in the back yard to play just doesn't cut it. Taking long walks, jogging, and playing interactively with you—fetching a tennis ball or chasing a Frisbee—are musts if you want your dog to be physically and emotionally healthy.

What Not to Do

Never hit your dog. It's never okay to beat a dog—with anything—or to hurt him by stepping on his feet, kneeing him in the chest, kicking him, or using a device such as a cattle prod. It sounds awful, but believe it or not, these are some of the ways people deal with aggression. Such actions are not only wrong, they're dangerous, and can easily make the problem worse.

What's the Prognosis?

How successful is treatment for aggression? It really depends a lot on how much of an effort you're willing to make. Treating aggression requires not only time but also the willingness to change your own behavior as well as your dog's. It also requires you to accept that your dog is always going to be at risk for aggressive behavior. There's no easy way around it: A dog who has a habit of biting can be made safer to be around, but there's no guarantee that she will never bite again. And treatment for ragelike behavior—described as unpredictable, impulsive, or sudden—is less likely to be successful.

Nonetheless, aggressive dogs can often be helped. By consistently ignoring unwanted behavior and rewarding good behavior, you can teach your dog how to live happily in the home, and the two of you can develop a mutually trusting relationship.

Kim Campbell Thornton is an award-winning writer and editor. During her tenure as editor of *Dog Fancy*, the magazine won three Dog Writers Association of America Maxwell Awards for best all-breed magazine. Her book *Why Do Cats Do That?* was named best behavior book in 1997 by the Cat Writers Association. Kim is the author of *Barking*, *Chewing*, *Digging*, *House-Training*, and *Aggression*. She serves on the DWAA Board of Governors and on the board of the Dog Writers Educational Trust. She is also the former president of the Cat Writers Association.

Buck Jones's humorous illustrations have appeared in numerous magazines (including *Dog Fancy* and *Cat Fancy*) and books. He is the illustrator for the best-selling books *Barking*, *Chewing*, *Digging*, *House-Training*, *Aggression*, *Why Do Cockatiels Do That?*, *Why Do Parakeets Do That?*, *Kittens! Why Do They Do What They Do?*, and *Puppies! Why Do They Do What They Do?*.